FOSSIL FILES

MAMMAL
FOSSILS

DANIELLE HAYNES

PowerKiDS
press™

NEW YORK

Published in 2017 by The Rosen Publishing Group, Inc.
29 East 21st Street, New York, NY 10010

First Edition

Editor: Melissa Raé Shofner
Book Design: Tanya Dellaccio

Photo Credits: Cover CM Dixon/Print Collector/Getty Images; cover, back cover, p. 1 Victoria Kalinina/Shutterstock.com; p. 5 Sylvain Sonnet/Getty Images; p. 7 (wolf and wolf pups) Geoffrey Kuchera/Shutterstock.com; p. 7 (echidna) Shutterstock.com; p. 9 John Phillips/UK Press/Getty Images; p. 10 Nada B/Shutterstock.com; p. 11 Ira Block/Getty Images; p. 13 (dinosaur bones) MyLoupe/ UIG/Getty Images; p. 13 corlaffra/Shutterstock.com; p. 15 (whale skeleton) Juergen Ritterbach/Getty Images; p. 15 (*megazostrodon*) Nicolas Primola/Shutterstock.com; p. 17 Natursports/Shutterstock.com; p. 19 Colin Keates/Getty Images; p. 21 covenant/Shutterstock.com; p. 23 Jonathan Blair/Getty Images; p. 25 (Lucy rendering) Dave Einsel/Stringer/Getty Images; p. 25 (Lucy bone fragments) Craig Hartley/ Bloomberg/Getty Images; p. 27 (*ulintatherium*) Florilegius/SSPL/Getty Images; p. 27 (Musem of Natural History) https://commons.wikimedia.org/wiki/File:USA-NYC-American_Museum_of_Natural_ History.JPG; p. 29 Rich Koele/Shutterstock.com; p. 30 Paul B. Moore/Shutterstock.com.

Library of Congress Cataloging-in-Publication Data

Names: Haynes, Danielle, author.
Title: Mammal fossils / Danielle Haynes.
Description: New York : PowerKids Press, [2017] | Series: Fossil files
Identifiers: LCCN 2016042593| ISBN 9781499427431 (pbk. book) | ISBN
  9781508152712 (6 pack) | ISBN 9781499428599 (library bound book)
Subjects: LCSH: Mammals, Fossil–Juvenile literature. |
  Mammals–Evolution–Juvenile literature. | Fossils–Juvenile literature. |
  Paleontology–History–Juvenile literature.
Classification: LCC QE881 .H39 2017 | DDC 569–dc23
LC record available at https://lccn.loc.gov/2016042593

Manufactured in the United States of America

CPSIA Compliance Information: Batch Batch #BW17PK: For Further Information contact Rosen Publishing, New York, New York at 1-800-237-9932

CONTENTS

MAMMAL RELATIVES

There are many different kinds of mammals living on Earth today. There are leopards prowling in the jungles, sea lions swimming in the oceans, and dogs and cats living in our homes with us. Even humans are mammals.

If you look far enough back in time, all true mammals share a common relative: a small, ratlike creature with a long, furry tail. If all mammals are related, why are some mammal species today so different from one another when other mammal species are so similar?

Scientists called paleontologists study fossils to discover how organisms evolved, or changed over time. By looking at mammal fossils, they learn how animals today share common ancestors and are more alike than you may think.

Are Humans Monkeys?

Humans didn't **evolve** from monkeys, but they do share a common ancestor with them. Between 5 million and 8 million years ago, that common ancestor evolved into two different **lineages**. One lineage eventually became humans and the other became apes such as gorillas, bonobos, orangutans, and gibbons. After the split, the human lineage evolved to include a number of species. Studying fossils helps scientists learn about the evolution that led to modern humans.

Some of the biggest mammal fossils are from mammoths. This mammoth skeleton is housed at the American Museum of Natural History in New York City.

WHAT IS A MAMMAL?

Animals with backbones are called vertebrates. A vertebrate can be placed into one of five groups based on its features. The five groups are: amphibians, birds, fish, mammals, and reptiles. Here, we'll focus on mammals.

If you have a dog or cat at home, you likely already know some of the features of mammals. In addition to a backbone, all mammals have fur or hair at some point in their life. Believe it or not, even dolphins have whiskers, or hair that grows near their mouth. These whiskers fall out soon after a dolphin is born. Mammals are warm-blooded, which means they can maintain their own body heat even when it's cold outside. Female mammals feed their young milk produced by their bodies. Most mammals give birth to live young.

You can tell a wolf is a mammal because it's covered in fur, has a backbone, and feeds its pups milk.

echidna

Mammals That Don't Act Like Mammals

Some animals don't seem like they're mammals even though they really are. Most mammals give birth to live young, but there are a few that lay eggs. Mammals that lay eggs, such as the platypus and echidna, are called monotremes. Some marine mammals may not seem to have much in common with other mammals. However, whales and porpoises do, in fact, have a small bit of hair. They're also warm-blooded and give birth to live young.

WHAT IS A FOSSIL?

Fossils are the preserved remains of organisms that once lived on Earth. There are two types: body fossils and trace fossils. Body fossils are made of or from the bones, teeth, skin, or hair of an animal. Sometimes whole organisms are found. They're often preserved in rock or frozen in ice. Scientists have even found whole insects and other small creatures preserved in **amber**.

The footprints or tracks from an organism's dragging tail or belly can also be preserved. These are called trace fossils. Trace fossils show the activity of an organism.

For the preserved remains or traces of a plant or animal to be considered a fossil, they must be at least 10,000 years old. The oldest fossils date back to 3.7 billion years ago.

Dig It!

Even the poop of long-dead animals can be a fossil. Paleontologists study fossilized dung—called coprolite—to learn what prehistoric animals ate and what kinds of illnesses they had.

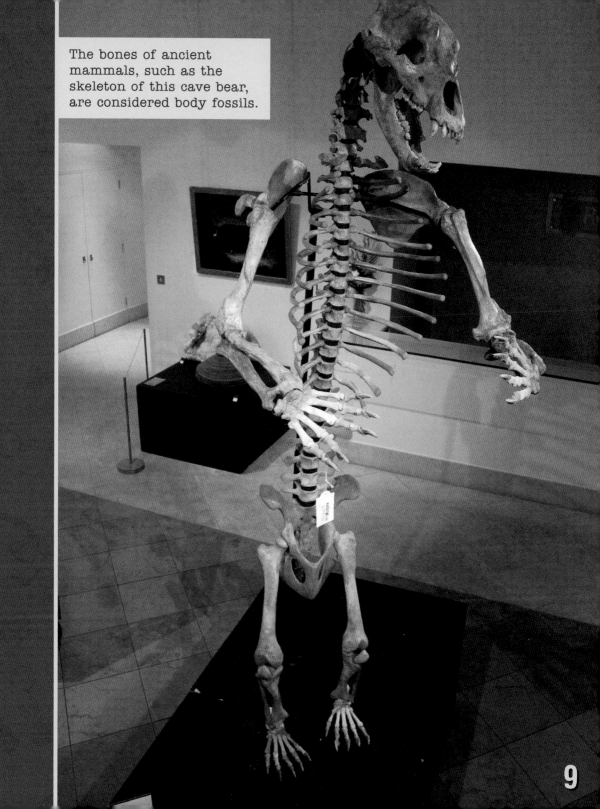

The bones of ancient mammals, such as the skeleton of this cave bear, are considered body fossils.

FOSSIL FORMATION

Fossils are formed in several different ways. Usually, the softer parts of an organism's body are the fastest parts to decompose, or break down. Many fossils are made up of just the hard parts of an organism, such as its bones, shell, or teeth. Most organisms completely decompose before they can be preserved. In some cases, though, nature stops decomposition and creates a fossil.

After an organism dies, its remains may be covered with **sediment**. This protects the remains from hungry animals and the weather. The organism's soft body parts eventually break down, and its bones are replaced by rock.

fossilzed mammoth tooth

This early horse lived during the Eocene epoch, about 56 million to 34 million years ago. Based on the fish fossils nearby, this horse likely died in the water.

DIGGING DEEPER

Paleontologists can make guesses about how old a fossil is based on the layer of rock in which it's found. It took many years for each rock layer to form. An existing layer of the earth would slowly be covered with a new layer of lava or sediment. The bodies of dead organisms would be covered up as the layers formed. If an organism's body was in a sediment layer, its remains may have become a fossil.

Scientists know that fossils found in deeper layers of rock must be from an older time period than those found higher up. Fossils from a particular layer of rock are believed to be from the same time period as other fossils found in the same layer.

Dig It!

Sedimentary rock is made up of horizontal, or flat, layers, but sometimes you might see slanted, or angled, layers. Slanted layers occur when Earth's crust moves and the land is pushed up or down.

In some sedimentary rock, you can see the layers very clearly. The fossils of animals and plants were preserved within these layers as they hardened into rock.

WHEN DO MAMMALS FIT IN?

Earth formed about 4.6 billion years ago. Its history is divided into different time periods. The earliest fossils are of bacteria that lived about 3.7 billion years ago.

These early life-forms evolved over time. Mammals first started appearing on Earth around 250 million years ago, during the Triassic period. They existed at the same time as dinosaurs. *Megazostrodon*, a small creature that looked like a shrew, was one of the first mammals.

Early mammals were fairly small. They didn't evolve to be bigger until after dinosaurs went extinct around 65 million years ago. About 60 million years ago, the variety of mammals on Earth greatly increased. *Homo sapiens*, or modern humans, came into being around 190,000 years ago.

Megazostrodon

Hundreds of fossils of some of the earliest forms of whales have been found at the Wadi al-Hitan site in Egypt. Wadi al-Hitan translates to "whale valley."

COLLECTING FOSSILS

Mammal fossils have been found on all seven continents. Most are buried under many layers of dirt and rock, which makes them hard to remove. Paleontologists use a variety of tools to dig out fossils. They use different tools depending on the size and location of a fossil. Scientists may need to use construction equipment to dig out **specimens** located deep underground.

Once most of the rock surrounding a fossil has been removed, smaller tools such as picks, hammers, and brushes are used. These tools allow paleontologists to carefully remove dirt and stone from around a fossil without damaging it. After they're removed from the ground, fossils are protected with plaster and padding so they can be safely moved to a museum or laboratory for further study.

These paleontologists are working at a dig site in Spain. Fossils and stone tools made by early humans have been found here.

HIGH-TECH BONES

New **technology** helps paleontologists learn even more from fossils. Computer-aided **X-ray** scans allow scientists to look at fossils without having to cut into them or even remove them from the earth. Using these scans, scientists can see what an animal ate right before it died and also look inside its cells. These scans can give scientists enough information to create a physical model of a prehistoric animal.

In 2010, scientists were looking for fish fossils in Madagascar. They took a large piece of stone back to their lab for further study. When they scanned the stone, they saw a skull inside. The skull belonged to a new mammal species, which the scientists named *Vintana sertichi*. Scientists determined that these giant, groundhog-like creatures lived between 72 million and 66 million years ago.

Diprotodon resembled a wombat and was the largest marsupial to ever live. Scientists used a medical scanner in a hospital to create digital images of *Diprotodon's* skull and find out more about how it bit into things.

THE OLDEST TRUE MAMMAL

In 2010, paleontologists discovered one of the oldest ever mammal fossils in eastern China. Scientists named the fossilized creature *Juramaia sinensis*. Its fossil is thought to be about 160 million years old. This makes it about 35 million years older than the next oldest "true mammal" fossil ever found.

A true mammal gives birth to fully **developed** babies. Marsupials, another kind of mammal, have babies that must develop more in their mothers' stomach pouch after they're born. Kangaroos are modern marsupials.

True mammals and marsupials shared a common mammal ancestor during the Jurassic period, but over time the lineage split as they developed different features. The discovery and study of the shrewlike *Juramaia sinensis* fossil tells researchers this split happened earlier than they first believed.

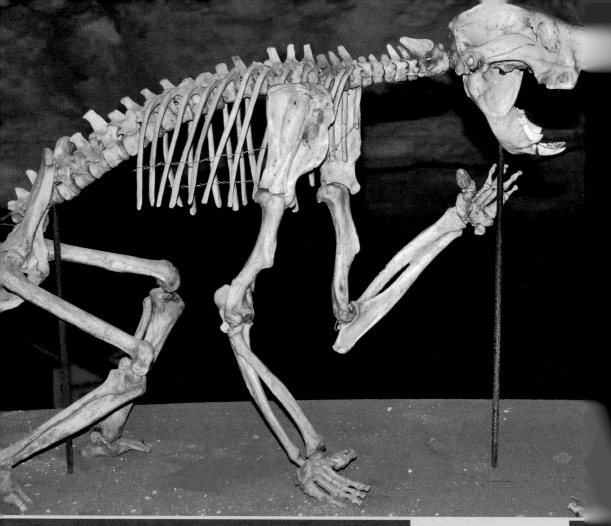

Dig It!

What is a scientific name? It's a Latin name used by scientists to identify an organism. This name is different from the common name we use to describe an organism. For example, the scientific name

Thylacoleo carnifex was the largest carnivorous marsupial alive during the Pliocene epoch (5.3 million to 2.6 million years ago) in what is now Australia. It may have hunted other giant mammals such as *Diprotodon*.

MESSEL SHALE PIT

There are some sites in the world that are particularly well known for being rich with well-preserved fossils. One is the Messel shale pit in southwest Germany. So many fossils have been found here that it's been added to the United Nations' World Heritage List. This means the area is protected because of its historical value.

The fossils found in the Messel shale pit are from the Eocene epoch. They're between 57 million and 36 million years old. These fossils provide paleontologists with information about the early stages of mammal evolution.

Some of the mammal fossils found in the pit belonged to a species of early horse relatives. *Propalaeotherium* likely weighed only 22 pounds (10 kg). The fossils of these small horse relatives were so well preserved, scientists found ancient berries in their stomachs.

Dig It!

Other World Heritage sites rich in mammal fossils include Riversleigh and Naracoorte in Australia.

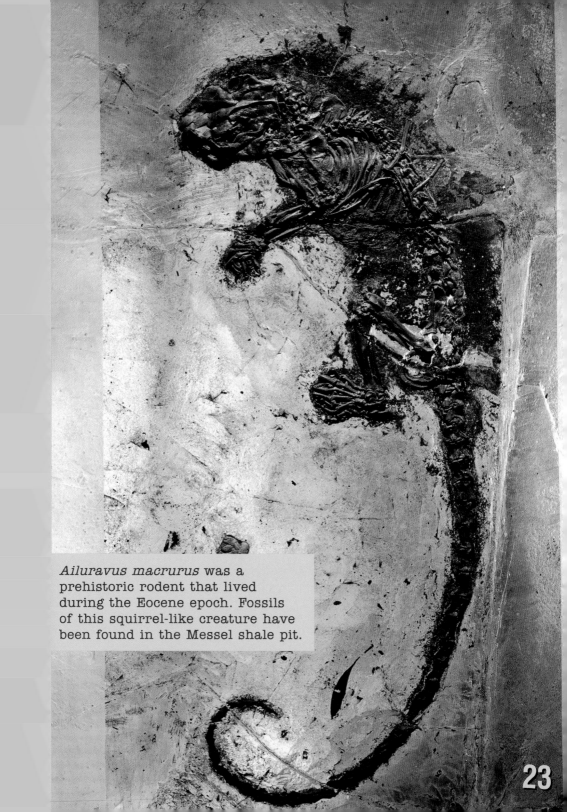

Ailuravus macrurus was a prehistoric rodent that lived during the Eocene epoch. Fossils of this squirrel-like creature have been found in the Messel shale pit.

HUMAN RELATIVE FOSSILS

Fossil discoveries sometimes have a big effect on how scientists understand modern human diseases and biology. In 2016, a team of scientists in South Africa found a fossil bone from a human relative with traces of **cancer**. They believed it to be the oldest example of cancer in a fossil of a human relative. The scientists determined the fossil was 1.7 million years old. This was much older than the next-oldest specimen, which was only 120,000 years old.

The discovery of this fossil was important because it challenged the idea that cancers are only caused by modern lifestyles. This includes the things that humans today eat and drink and the types of chemicals we are exposed to. Our early human relatives wouldn't have been exposed to the same things.

Lucy, an example of *Australopithecus afarensis*, is one of the most famous **hominin** fossils ever found. Pieces of her 3.2-million-year-old skull and skeleton were found in Ethiopia in 1974.

THE BONE WARS

One of the largest collections of mammal fossils is found at the American Museum of Natural History in New York City. The museum has about 400,000 specimens representing 7,599 different mammal species.

A large number of these specimens came from the collection of 19th-century paleontologist E. D. Cope. Cope's interest in collecting prehistoric fossils led him to travel all over the American West in search of previously undiscovered species.

A rivalry with fellow paleontologist O. C. Marsh started what has since been nicknamed the "Bone Wars." Each man wanted to make more fossil discoveries than the other. Marsh even sent spies to keep an eye on Cope's research. The rivalry hurt each man's **reputation** in the field of paleontology and both died nearly penniless.

Ulintatherium lived 56 million to 33.9 million years ago. E. D. Cope's collection contained fossils of these prehistoric mammals.

American Museum of Natural History

Dig It!

E. D. Cope sold part of his fossil collection to the American Museum of Natural History for $32,000 in 1897. Today, this would be nearly

STUDYING FOSSILS

There are many career paths for young people interested in paleontology. If you'd like to work in the field, make sure to take plenty of STEM (science, technology, **engineering**, and math) classes in school. You should also study history and other social sciences. Many jobs in paleontology require a college degree in biology, which is the science of life. It's also important to study geology, the science of the earth, since you'll need to know about rock layers.

Some paleontologists have more than one job. Some teach classes at a university during the school year and spend the summers in the field, digging up bones. Other paleontologists work in museums or at scientific research centers using microscopes and high-tech equipment to study fossil specimens.

Amateur Fossil Hunting

Fossil hunting isn't just for the professionals. Anyone can grab a shovel and brush and start their very own fossil collection. The Peace River campground in southwest Florida welcomes inexperienced fossil hunters. The Peace River is a freshwater river, but the area was once part of a shallow sea. Shark teeth are a common find there. However, in 1996, someone found a nearly complete fossilized Columbian mammoth, which is a mammal.

Columbian mammoths lived across North America, from Canada down to central Mexico.

Studying mammal fossils is a great way to learn about Earth's ancient history. By studying fossils, scientists have been able to figure out how animals that lived millions of years ago adapted to survive or went extinct. Adaptations give scientists clues about how the climate has changed over time. The information that scientists collect about our human ancestors helps us understand the biology, illnesses, and evolution of modern-day humans.

The best part about fossils is that you don't have to be a paleontologist to go looking for them. Are there any public fossil-hunting areas near where you live? What can some of the specimens you find there tell you about the ancient history of your region? Maybe you could make a mammal fossil discovery!

GLOSSARY

amber: A hardened type of tree resin.

cancer: A sickness in which cells multiply out of control and do not work properly.

develop: The act of building, creating, changing, or growing over time.

engineering: The study and practice of using math and science to do useful things, such as building machines.

evolve: To grow and change over time.

hominin: A member of a group that includes both *Homo sapiens* (or modern-day humans) and extinct members of the human lineage.

lineage: A group of organisms that can trace their descent from a common ancestor.

reputation: The views that are held about something or someone.

sediment: Matter such as rocks, sand, and stones that is moved and deposited by water, wind, or glaciers.

specimen: A sample that is selected for examination, study, or display, usually chosen as typical of its kind.

technology: A method that uses science to solve problems and the tools used to solve those problems.

X-ray: A powerful type of energy that is similar to light but is invisible to the human eye.

INDEX

WEBSITES

Due to the changing nature of Internet links, PowerKids
Press has developed an online list of websites related to the
subject of this book. This site is updated regularly. Please use this
link to access the list: www.powerkidslinks.com/ff/mam